CW01163080

Original title:
The Winter Wind's Song

Copyright © 2024 Creative Arts Management OÜ
All rights reserved.

Author: Gabriel Kingsley
ISBN HARDBACK: 978-9916-94-600-8
ISBN PAPERBACK: 978-9916-94-601-5

The Sigh of Sleet and Silence

Sleet fell down with a clatter,
Making penguins dance and scatter.
My nose, it drips like a crazy tap,
I lost my hat in a snowy nap.

Frosty fingers, they pinch and tease,
Dogs skitter past with the greatest of ease.
Snowmen grin with carrot noses,
While icicles hang like frozen roses.

Echoing Shadows of Winter's Grip

In shadows deep where snowflakes play,
A squirrel chirps in the fanciest way.
He stole my snack, oh what a thief,
Now I chase him, he's causing grief.

The echo of laughter dances around,
As children tumble and roll to the ground.
But watch your step, it's slick and sly,
You'll end up laughing, if you slip and fly.

A Chord of Snowflakes and Silence

A snowflake falls, a delicate star,
It sticks to my tongue, oh how bizarre!
I'm trying to catch them, they swirl and spin,
But they melt too fast—where do I begin?

Silence reigns, then a snowball fight,
Laughter erupts, oh what a sight!
I took one shot, then stumbled down,
Now I'm the clown in this snowy town.

Voices Lost in the Frosted Air

Voices echo in the crisp, cold air,
A cat darts by with a frosty glare.
"Hey, human! Why'ya out at this hour?"
I swear she's judging my winter power!

The wind howls tunes of a silly song,
While penguins waddle, proud and strong.
We shimmy and shake in the frozen breeze,
In a world spun quiet, yet full of glee.

Lullaby of the Frozen Night

In the night so cold and bright,
Snowflakes dance in pure delight.
A penguin slips, his feet askew,
And mutters, "What's a bird to do?"

A squirrel darts, then tumbles down,
Wearing snow like a silly crown.
The moonlight glints on icicles,
While rabbits hop and make it tickle!

The whispers of the frosty breeze,
Tickle noses, bring us to our knees.
The bears all snore, but we just giggle,
As snowmen wobble and start to wiggle!

With cocoa dreams and marshmallow hats,
We dance with snowflakes, chitchat with cats.
So blame the cold for all this cheer,
We're all just nuts, when winter's near!

Ballad of the Shivering Trees

Oh, the trees do shake and shiver,
And here comes a squirrel to deliver.
He wears a scarf that's far too wide,
And keeps tripping – what a ride!

Branches creak with every gust,
As they murmur tales of winter's trust.
A fox rolls over in the snow,
And gives a yawn that's oh-so-slow.

Icicles dangle with a clink,
While birds in hats give us a wink.
A giggle echoes through the pines,
"Who's the fluffiest?" in hasty lines!

So grab your mittens, join the jig,
And twirl with trees that dance a gig.
It's icy fun, with frosty snaps,
In the shivering embrace of winter's laps!

Chilling Harmonies in the Dark

The night is cold, yet spirits soar,
As critters gather 'round to snore.
But one raccoon, with belly wide,
Plays the drums with a snowman's side!

The moonlight forms a shiny band,
With frosty notes across the land.
While owls provide a hoot and holler,
Two ice skates snug, they twist and baller.

The shadows dance with giddy glee,
As laughter bubbles, wild and free.
A hare sings high, while badgers snore,
Their winter concert, we adore!

In chilling tunes, we find our sway,
With notes like snowflakes on display.
Under starlit skies, we all unite,
To sing our jolly tunes tonight!

Frosty Ballads in the Twilight

The twilight brings a frosty gleam,
As penguins plot a winter dream.
They slide and slip, a lively crew,
In snowball fights, their spirits flew!

A hoot from owls with muffled toes,
While a frozen critter tightly doze.
The snowdrops giggle, as they sway,
In dreams of snowmen gone astray!

A snowflake lands upon a nose,
Causing sneezes, laughter flows.
The chill's a joker, dressed in white,
While critters jive in frosty light!

So join the fun and let it ring,
With playful chills and laughs we bring.
For every tear from icy bliss,
Is just a smile in winter's kiss!

Flickering Shadows of Frost

In the town square, we all gather,
To hear the giggles of snow and chatter.
Frosty flakes dance, a clumsy ballet,
As snowmen wobble and fall in dismay.

Snowball fights commence with great glee,
But watch out, here comes that sneaky bee!
A mistletoe prank hangs low on the tree,
And laughter erupts like a wild jubilee.

Hot cocoa spills—who needs a cup?
Just wear your marshmallows, mix it up!
Sleds race down the hills with a thud,
And cheeks turn red like a ripe, juicy bud.

Pine trees dress up in fluffy white coats,
As we slide in our slick winter boats.
Oh, the tickle of frost and a slip on the ice,
Winter games are clumsy, oh so nice!

Cadence of Stillness Under Snow

Snowflakes swirl as if in a dance,
But a twist of the foot makes you lose your stance.
Chasing each other, slipping all around,
Falling like popcorn, spreading joy abound.

Mittens mismatched, and scarves all askew,
A parade of penguins, just me and you.
But oh, what's that? A squirrel on a spree,
Stealing our snacks, oh, how could it be?

Ice cubes clink in glasses, cheers in the air,
For a snowball soup, served with a flair.
The dog shows off, slips, then takes a dive,
His wagging tail says, "I'm still alive!"

Huddled around, our laughter must flow,
As the moon beams down on the frosty glow.
In this frosty lull, we'll sing without shame,
For winter's spirit is a kooky game!

Tale of the Cold Embrace

Once upon a time, in a land of white,
A penguin slipped—oh, what a sight!
He took a tumble with flair and grace,
While polar bears chuckled, "What a race!"

A snowman named Frosty felt quite spry,
Until a warm hug made him sigh.
With a grin made of carrots, he tried to flee,
But melted away with a giggle and glee.

Icicles dangled, sharp as a wink,
Making snowflakes giggle on the brink.
As laughter echoes in the frosty air,
We embrace the cold, without a care.

Chilling breezes whisper secrets untold,
With frostbitten toes, we laugh and behold.
So here's to winter, a quirky affair,
Where each frozen moment's a reason to share!

Frosty Knell in the Night

Beneath a blanket of shimmering frost,
We dance to the tunes of the snow's soft cost.
A howl in the distance, perhaps a prank,
The moon lights the way with its silvery flank.

The rabbit hops high, what a funny show,
As it tumbles and rolls in the fluffy snow.
With each little leap, a chuckle we find,
Nature's own jester, one of a kind.

Chilly winds whistle a discordant song,
While yo-yoing snowflakes just skip along.
They swirl like leaves, but in layers so cold,
It's a frosty knell that never gets old.

So gather 'round, friends, for this wintry jive,
Where laughter and snowflakes keep us alive.
Amidst the moonlight and a blanket of white,
We celebrate coziness, sweet quirks of the night!

Journey of the Icy Whispers

Through frostbitten trees, the whispers flee,
Laughing at snowmen who spill their tea.
Chasing squirrels in hats, all decked out,
They tickle the noses of those who pout.

With icy giggles, they twirl and spin,
Causing the mailman to slip with a grin.
They poke and they prod at every lost shoe,
While frosty flakes fall, they're laughing too!

A frosty parade in a jolly sense,
Hiding behind every tall, snow-clad fence.
Each flake's a joke, a plucky little sprite,
Sending the sledders into pure fright!

So come take a ride on the frosty breeze,
Join the giggles of shadows beneath the trees.
For when icy whispers have something to say,
You'll find tons of laughter along the way.

Glistening Dreams in the Chill

Glimmers and sparkles on branches aglow,
The trees are just laughing at all the snow.
They shimmy and shake with a twinkle and chime,
While dancing around like they've lost track of time.

Snowflakes are falling, they flurry and swoosh,
Poking out tongues for a playful old woosh.
Icicles hang like the funniest teeth,
Making the houses look quite like a wreath.

With every gust, a chuckle ensues,
As critters slide past in their brand-new shoes.
Frosty giggles in crystalline air,
Each snowmen's face wears a silly old stare.

So prance through the fields with a hop and a skip,
Join in the fun, get a frosty small dip.
For in this chill, love the laughter and dreams,
As winter unfolds with its glistening schemes.

Voice of the Wintry Ghosts

A voice in the briskness sends shivers and chills,
As snowflakes perform on the frosty hill.
They giggle and sigh, those phantom-like forms,
While battling snowballs in swirling storms.

With howls of delight, they rattle the trees,
Tickling the critters, bringing them to knees.
Their icicle chains jingle, delightfully bright,
As they race down the lane in the pale moonlight.

Adjacent to laughter are whispers and cheers,
For they know that winter is fun for the years.
So venture outside, join the merry band,
And let the embracing cold give you a hand!

In this trackless night, let the spirits ignite,
With joyous tomfoolery wrapped up so tight.
The ghostly refrain will dance and will jest,
Carving smiles in the snow as they put you to the test.

Wistful Echoes of the North

When echoes of laughter drift over the hills,
A chorus of chuckles, it surely instills.
With snowdrifts piled high, making cushions so sweet,
Kids tumble and roll, wiggling their feet.

The north winds conspire to tickle your nose,
With skidding and slipping that nobody knows.
Each house wears a blanket of shimmering white,
While shadows perform in the pale twilight.

As frost paints the world, bringing magic around,
Little creatures are stirring, making delightful sound.
Each soft sway of branches brings whispers of fun,
While everyone's searching for snowball to run.

So let giggles ring out in the freezing air tight,
While we prance in the snow until day turns to night.
For wistful echoes from the heart will ignite,
A season of joy in the chilling moonlight.

Serenade of Snowflakes

Snowflakes tumble down like fools,
Dancing on rooftops, ignoring the rules.
They tickle your nose and cover your toes,
Whispering secrets that nobody knows.

They gather in heaps, a soft, furry law,
Making snowmen who'll never withdraw.
With buttons for eyes and a carrot for flair,
They crack silly jokes to the frosty air.

Caught in a flurry, they whirl and spin,
Bouncing on strangers with a cheeky grin.
They steal all the warmth, like a winter heist,
While everyone dodges them, giggling, amused.

So here's to the snowflakes, a merry band,
Bringing laughter and chaos across the land.
With a twirl and a spin, they scatter and splay,
Like tiny comedians dashing away.

Dance of the Antarctic Breath

The chilled gusts arrive with a comical flair,
Twirling the hats off folks unaware.
With a whoosh and a puff, they cause quite a scene,
As mittens take flight, like they're part of a dream.

Penguins waddle by, quite clumsy and bright,
Slipping and sliding, what a hilarious sight!
They slide on their bellies, whirling with glee,
In a dance that is far from a simple decree.

As icebergs loom large, they bob and they sway,
While polar bears chuckle, come join in the play.
With each gust of wind, there's a giggle or two,
As frosty fun erupts from the chilly blue.

So let's raise a toast to this frosty ballet,
Where the air is alive, and it's all here to stay.
Embrace the eccentric, the silly, the bold,
For winter's strange dance is a joy to behold!

Murmurs Beneath the Ice

Under the ice, a giggle does glide,
With whispers of snowflakes, our frosty hide.
They snicker at penguins, who trip on the shore,
While fish in the sea conduct an encore.

The seals crack jokes in their fluffy attire,
As snowballs fly high, fueled by their fire.
'The water is warm!' they quip with delight,
While frostbitten toes dance in chilly night.

In the depths, a choir of icicles sing,
Tickling the underbelly of winter's fling.
All nature joins in for a cold, frosty jest,
As shivers and laughter intertwine at their fest.

So heed the whispers beneath winter's embrace,
For beneath icy layers, there's joy to trace.
With chilly chuckles and frozen surprise,
Embrace the giggles that cold days can prize.

Chords of the Frigid Air

Frosty flutes play, as the cold winds collide,
Composing a symphony we cannot abide.
With each note that travels, it tickles the crowd,
Creating a melody jocular and loud.

Icicles twinkle, like lights in a show,
As air takes a bow, then twirls to and fro.
The trees clap their branches, a raucous affair,
While snow forts emerge, creating the dare.

Beneath the bright moon, the laughter does swell,
With snowball duels breaking out, oh so well!
The cold kisses playfulness into the night,
As winter's own concert brings sheer delight.

So cherish these chords beneath blankets of white,
For winter's a joker, bringing frosty delight.
When laughter is shared in the chill of the air,
Every icy moment transforms into flair.

Lament of the Frosted Earth

A snowman lost his carrot nose,
He sneezed and blew it off, I suppose!
With frosty breath, he starts to pout,
'Where's my snack? I'm in a drought!'

The icy ground cracks like a joke,
A squirrel in boots begins to croak.
He slips and slides, oh what a sight,
Dancing like a star on a winter night.

Clouds are fluffy, like cotton candy,
But cold snaps make us all feel dandy.
Hot cocoa mugs we raise and cheer,
For laughter echoes, winter's here!

In the chill, we play and shout,
With snowball fights, we toss about.
Each flurry brings a grin so wide,
A frosty funfair, our hearts abide.

Echoing Whispers of Winter

The crunch of snow beneath my feet,
A ridiculous ballet, oh what a feat!
With each little slip, I can't help but smile,
Like a walrus trying to walk a mile.

A penguin waddle down the lane,
With fluffy hats that seem insane.
They trip and tumble, what a show,
Winter leaves us laughing, don't you know?

Frosty breath like dragon's flame,
The cold is quirky, what a game!
We build a fort, the best in town,
With pillows and laughter, we won't frown.

Gloves and mittens, mismatched pair,
A fashion statement beyond compare.
In this frosty fun, we prance,
Winter's a reason to dance and dance!

Song of the Shivering Moonlight

Beneath the moon, the world huddles tight,
A penguin's waddle is quite the sight!
With icy jokes, the stars conspire,
To make us laugh around the fire.

The frosty trees, where snowflakes cling,
Look like they've had one too many drinks!
They sway and stumble in a merry dance,
Inviting all for a frosty prance.

Mittens fly with daring zest,
Snowball fights that never rest.
The chilly air, a friend so dear,
Each icy chuckle brighten the atmosphere.

As blankets of snow cover the ground,
Silly snowmen wobble around.
With every gust, our spirits rise,
In wintry glee, we reach for the skies!

Noteworthy Chill of the Ether

Oh, the frost bites with a giggling grin,
While we sip hot cocoa, let the fun begin!
An avalanche of laughter, snowflakes collide,
Like clowns on a hill, we slide side by side.

The frost paints windows, a silvery mess,
Each splotch a story of winter's excess.
With mismatched socks, we dash and run,
In this frozen land, we laugh and have fun.

From rooftops, icicles dangle and sway,
Like toothy grins that brighten the day.
We toss our hats, let the giggles flow,
In winter's shenanigans, joy starts to grow.

Peeking out from my warm, cozy nook,
I spy a snowball—time for the hook!
With joyful yells, we cheerfully fight,
For in this chilly play, we find pure delight.

Secrets of the Frozen Gust

A snowman grins with a carrot nose,
Waving his arms as the cold wind blows.
He tells the tales of slippery floors,
And how no one should wear woolly drawers!

The frosty breeze steals hats with glee,
While giggling squirrels sip iced tea.
With a frosty laugh, they play their game,
As snowflakes fall and join the fame!

Snowflakes dance like sprightly sprites,
Causing snowball fights on winter nights.
With laughter echoing through the trees,
Even icicles drip in a breeze!

Each gust brings tickles and frosty fun,
Chasing children 'til they run.
The secrets of cold air, so well known,
Make winter feel like a comedy zone!

Soft Echoes in the Frozen Wood

In chillier woods, a critter sneezes,
Scaring a deer who jumps and flees.
Branches creak as they freeze,
While frosty squirrels chow on cheese.

Snowflakes whisper like cheeky friends,
Telling secrets that never ends.
A chilly chorus, oh what a tune,
As winter laughs beneath the moon!

Critters skate on frozen ponds,
While a snowman vexes with his wands.
With his broom, he sweeps up giggles,
As snowballs fly, and laughter wiggles!

Echoes soft in the frozen trees,
Mice can't stop shaking their knees.
Winter's hilarity, ice-bound and bright,
Turns every cold day into pure delight!

Tale of the Whispering Frost

A feathered friend in a snowy coat,
Tells of a cat who thinks he can float.
He leapt and slipped on a patch of ice,
Landing in snow, and oh, what a slice!

Whispers swirl in the frosty air,
As snowflakes tease with mischievous flair.
They tickle noses, and cheeks grow red,
As giggles erupt from every kid's head!

Frozen ponds turn into playful scenes,
Where penguin dances fill the gleans.
With every tumble, a chorus of laughs,
As winter's chill gives us all good gaffs!

A tale unfolds beneath starry skies,
With snowmen plotting and raccoon spies.
Through the whispers of winter's might,
Every side-eyes, and joy takes flight!

Riddle of the Icy Gale

The icy gale plays tricks on you,
Like how scarves can magically flew.
A slap of chill, a giggle here,
As hats take off in a dance of cheer!

What's round and white but fun to fling?
A snowball, yes! Let's hear them sing!
The answers pending in frosty air,
As laughter erupts everywhere!

Beneath the frost, a mischief brews,
Snowflakes grin with their chilly hues.
A riddle spun with tingly delight,
As friends unite in the snowy night!

The question lingers in breezy trails,
What makes winter a time of tales?
With playful hearts feeling so bold,
The answer, dear friend, is laughter retold!

Frosty Twilight Serenade

In the cold, a sneeze does bloom,
Snowflakes dance and greet the gloom.
Puffy coats and hats so wide,
Laughing as my nose does slide.

Icicles hang like frozen spears,
Each gust whispers tales of cheers.
Hot cocoa steams with marshmallow hugs,
While snowmen wear carrot mugs.

Socks go missing, but who's to blame?
Chasing warmth, it's a silly game.
Slipping on ice, it's pure delight,
In this chilly, frosty flight.

Caress of the Wintry Dusk

Frosty breath in the chilly air,
Snowball fights without a care.
Woolly mittens go flying high,
As laughter echoes from the sky.

Chasing shadows on the ground,
With every slip, we spin 'round.
Frosty noses and cheeks that glow,
In this snowy, frosty show.

Snowmen frown when hat winds lift,
A snowflake's dance is quite the gift.
With every gust, the giggles bloom,
As winter turns the world to zoom.

Reverberations of the Glacial Whisper

A frosty breeze brings dancing feet,
Where snowflakes play a chilly beat.
Sledding down hills, we scream with glee,
Riding frozen waves of jubilee.

Pine trees dressed in coats of white,
Whisper secrets late at night.
Hot drinks spill as we take a sip,
While laughter makes the moment flip.

Snowball fights turn into truce,
With winter's magic, we let loose.
In chilly air, our joy takes flight,
Under stars twinkling bright.

Anthem of the Chilly Gale

Gusty breaths make hats take flight,
Chasing them leads to pure delight.
Laughing hard with frosty breath,
In this chill, we dance with death.

Snowflakes tickle as they land,
Sleds go crashing, oh so grand.
Winter games bring friends so near,
With jolly fun, we have no fear.

Mittens soggy from playful throws,
Colors bright like winter shows.
The chilly gale steals our hats,
But we chase after, like playful cats.

Cadence of the Howling Storm

A howl through the trees, oh what a delight,
Even the squirrels scurry left and right.
The snowflakes dance with a giggling cheer,
Frosty noses freeze, but we persevere.

With hats on our heads, we wobble and slide,
As gusts pull our scarves like a mischievous tide.
Laughter erupts as we tumble and fall,
The storm sings a tune, a comical call.

Footprints follow where two penguins waddle,
Each step's a new story, join in the prattle.
As chattering teeth join in on the fun,
We chase after snowmen, all but a run!

So let the storm dance; let the winds blow free,
With cheeks rosy red, we're as happy as can be.
Snowballs are flying, it's chaos in bloom,
In this silly rhythm, we banish the gloom.

Whispering Pines and Icy Auras

Pines whisper secrets, as giggles ensue,
They're snickering at us in shimmery dew.
The slippery path claims a slapstick show,
With each graceless stumble, we steal the snow's glow.

Icicles dangle, like frozen parade,
We swing our arms wildly, an icecapade trade.
Glares from the snowmen, their buttons aglow,
Are they judging our moves, or enjoying the show?

Hot cocoa in hand, but it's frozen and chill,
Each sip's like a snowball that gives us a thrill.
We toast to the gusts that rattle our hats,
And laugh with the pines, oh how they are brats!

Under the slippery sky, we giggle and slide,
With fluffy white pillows, we take on the ride.
From snowy tomfoolery, we never will part,
For fun in the cold is a warm, joyful heart.

Darkening Skies and Silver Lines

As shadows grow tall and the clouds start to twirl,
The sky plays a game, making our heads whirl.
A wink from the moon, like he's in on the fun,
As snowflakes descend, oh, where will they run?

Down in the valley, the critters just laugh,
Snowballs thrown wildly, what a silly gaffe!
Each tumble and trip, like a comic relief,
In the face of the storm, who needs belief?

A blizzard hugs tightly, then chaotically spins,
We're all in a whirl—where does this madness begin?
Snowman assemblies become winter's grand show,
With noses all crooked, they steal the snow's glow.

So here's to the shivers and laughter that ring,
Caught in the web of this whimsical fling.
With each frosty puffle, our smiles start to shine,
In darkening skies, we find the silver line.

Lonesome Calls of the Northern Gale

Oh, the gale calls my name, with a chuckle, it seems,
Drawing out snowflakes from laughter-filled dreams.
We shimmy and slide, the ice sings a tune,
While the night makes us dance beneath the cold moon.

The chill in the air is a cheeky old chap,
With frost on our toes, we're caught in a trap.
But who cares for frost? We're now in a play,
Each gust brings our giggles to lighten the gray.

Downhill we roll like the stars on a spree,
The snowmen start laughing, oh won't they agree?
With carrots for noses, they jest with delight,
In this lonesome gale, we're all here for a fight!

So here's to the chill, and to laughter's great art,
For winter's a canvas, and we play our part.
In the calls of the north, let our joy intertwine,
As we frolic and flourish, like the stars that align.

The Lure of the Bitter Breeze

A frosty breeze swept through my hair,
Making my nose feel quite the scare.
I tried to dance, but I lost my shoe,
Now it's frozen, but I still feel blue.

The snowflakes laugh as they twirl around,
I stumble and tumble, fall to the ground.
The ground is slippery, oh what a sight,
I should have stayed in, avoided this plight.

The trees all giggle with their frosty grace,
While I waddle and slip in a silly race.
The squirrels chuckle, holding their sides,
As I chase my own breath, on this icy slide.

So here's to cold, with a hearty cheer,
Though it's a blast, it's a bit severe.
With frozen fingers and snowflakes in tow,
Let's sip hot cocoa and bask in the glow.

Resounding Through the Frosted Landscape

In shorts and sandals, I stepped on out,
The snowflakes giggled, what's he about?
They swirled around me, their frosty breath,
Saying, "Good luck, you'll freeze to death!"

My nose became red, my cheeks turned pink,
Couldn't walk straight, tried not to sink.
I laughed at myself with each little slip,
What fun it is to go on this trip!

The snowmen waved with their carrot-nose smiles,
I joined the chaos, danced for a while.
They spun around with glee and delight,
I rolled in the snow, a comical sight.

With giggles and snickers echoing clear,
I may be silly, but I've got no fear.
For amidst all this frost, there's joy to find,
Embracing the chill, I leave worries behind.

Whispers of Frosted Breezes

Whispers of chill danced through the town,
As I slip on ice, fall straight down.
The marbles I lost from my pockets last night,
Are they frozen or just giving me fright?

Snowflakes are plotting, oh what a game,
Targeting heads, they aim for my name.
I dodge and I duck, but I can't complain,
For warmth from my cocoa is mine to gain.

Frosty friends tease with their icy tricks,
As I'm trying to figure out how to mix.
A little fun with each frozen step,
Marzipan snowballs, oh what a prep!

Laughter is louder than the chill in the air,
We dance in the snow without a single care.
So here's to the frost and the joy that it brings,
Dressed like a snowman, look at me bling!

Echoes of the Chilling Gale

The chilling gale gives a playful push,
As I twirl like a whirlwind, whoosh, whoosh, whoosh!
My scarf takes flight like a kite on a spree,
"Oh no!" I yell, "Come back, stay with me!"

The snowflakes whisper their frosty jive,
I'm juggling snowballs, feeling alive.
But somehow I trip, and down I go fast,
My landing? Impressive! Oh, what a blast!

The trees sway and chuckle, they know I'm a clown,
A frozen ballet in this white, frosty gown.
With each frosty gust, I'm grateful for cheer,
For laughter in winter is the best time of year.

So let's toast to the breeze, to the slips that we make,
With snowmen and giggles, our hearts never ache.
Let's sing with this chill, let our merriment flow,
In the echo of laughter, we watch winter glow!

Tales from the Snowy Gale

A snowman wobbles, round and tall,
His carrot nose begins to fall.
With every gust, he shakes and sways,
Just an icy puppet in the fray.

Squirrels scamper, tails held high,
In the frosty air, they leap and fly.
Chasing snowflakes, what a sight!
Little furballs in sheer delight.

Shovels squeak on icy streets,
Neighbors laugh, while winter greets.
Hot cocoa spills, and laughter spreads,
As snowballs fly, and joy embeds.

Late night carols, icy and bright,
Sing of snowmen who wobble with fright.
Under moonlight, they dance and prance,
In a whirlwind, they take a chance.

Chant of the Icebound Forest

Trees wear coats of frosty white,
Branches creaking, what a sight!
The owls hoot in muffled tones,
Lost in laughter, in frozen groans.

A bear with boots, oh what a show,
Slips on ice, puts on a toe.
He slides right past a snowy hare,
Both in giggles, without a care.

Snowflakes dance like tiny sprites,
Twirling around in frosty bites.
With each gust, they stumble and spin,
Kissing cheeks; let the fun begin!

Woodpeckers tap with sassy beats,
Knocking loudly, testing seats.
As frosty whispers fill the air,
It's a woodland ball, beyond compare.

Symphony of the Frozen Breeze

Icicles jingle like tiny bells,
As snowflakes waltz and twist like spells.
The snow plow honks and starts to groan,
While penguins slide and claim their throne.

Laughter echoes off icy walls,
In this season, mirth enthralls.
A polar bear wearing a scarf,
Struts through snow, trying to go far.

Frosty cheeks and noses red,
Playing games 'til ice is shed.
With every turn, a giggling sound,
As winter's song takes the ground.

In this frosty symphony we hear,
Jokes and laughter, full of cheer.
So let's sing loud, let's sing bright,
For winter's dance warms the night.

Chorus of the Frostbitten Air

The winds all whistle a cheeky tune,
While snowflakes drop like little balloons.
Hot chocolate spills on furry paws,
As laughter echoes, what a cause!

A gust blows brisk, it tickles the nose,
Making everyone's laughter grow.
Playful snowmen throw a snowball fight,
Under the stars, they beam so bright.

Chubby penguins march in a line,
All of them tasting the frosty wine.
Their waddle is quirky, a sight to see,
In this frozen land, wild and free.

So let's raise a glass to winter's charm,
In this chorus, no one's harmed.
For giggles and grins shall warm the air,
In this frosty wonder, everywhere!

Language of Crystallized Whispers

Snowflakes dance, a prance so neat,
Chasing squirrels, they skip and cheat.
Icicles hang like daggers bright,
Welcome to the chilly fight!

Frosty noses in the air,
Snowball battles go everywhere.
Laughter echoed on the slopes,
Frigid giggles; winter hopes!

A snowman wobbles, head askew,
'Tis hard to see when skies are blue!
Melting dreams dribble off his hat,
"Hey, someone save me!" He begged the cat.

Whispers flutter, frosty and shy,
In this season, we laugh and try.
Crystals swirl, a joke in play,
Winter's fun is here to stay!

Cry of the Frigid Twilight

Twilight arrives with a giggle and squeak,
Frosty critters peek from behind a creek.
"Hide and seek?" the squirrels declare,
As snowballs fly through the crisp, cold air.

Penguins waddle, boots twice their size,
Slipping on ice, what a funny surprise!
The moon is laughing, bobbing with glee,
While we freeze, sipping hot cocoa tea!

Gusty winds tell secrets so bold,
Whistling tales of snowmen old.
"Don't lose your hat!" they tease and shout,
As heads spin around, no doubt, no doubt!

In the twilight, warmth found in jokes,
Snowflakes giggle, just like folks.
They dance and swirl, in chill they play,
The frigid fun lights up the gray!

Singing Silence of the Northern Sky

Under the northern lights, we slide,
On frozen lakes, we laugh and glide.
Snowmen spin, arms outstretched wide,
While penguins giggle, quite dignified!

Stars twinkle bright, they shared a grin,
As snowflakes twirl, a joyful spin.
Every flake has a story to tell,
Of frosty dreams and winter's spell.

A frosty fox with a fluffy tail,
Sings to the moon, a tuneful wail.
What a sight, this chill so grand,
Even the snowmen join the band!

Hilarity reigns in the nighttime air,
As wintry spirits dance everywhere.
The silence is singing, quite out of tune,
Under the watch of a chuckling moon!

Sonata of the Snowman's Grief

A snowman sighs, with eyes of coal,
His carrot nose can't feel his role.
"Where's the sun?" he muses with dread,
"I'm melting here; I just made my bed!"

Snowflakes giggle, his plight is clear,
They spin in circles, "Don't shed a tear!"
Icicle tears hang from branches low,
While rabbits hop, putting on a show.

In this chilly mess, he starts to sway,
"Dance with me, friends, before it's my last day!"
Yet the warmth of laughter does not abide,
As chilly winds bring an icy tide.

Sighs in the snow, a sonata unsung,
While blizzard notes play, a tune has begun.
The snowman chuckles, it's not all dire,
In winter's embrace, there's warmth to inspire!

Hushed Moans of the Winter Night

Under the moon, the snowflakes twirl,
A chilly dance, not meant for girls.
They swirl and dip, oh what a sight,
As nose hairs freeze, I giggle at night.

Frosty whispers, they tease and play,
Making snowmen who wobble and sway.
Their carrot noses are slightly askew,
As they take a bow, adorned with the dew.

I trip on the ice, a comical fall,
Flailing like I'm a raggedy doll.
With each silly slip, laughter erupts,
Even the snow thinks I'm interrupting.

So here I sit, wrapped snug and tight,
Sharing my snacks with the snowman tonight.
For in this chill, joy fills my cup,
While winter's moans keep the giggles up.

Frozen Cadenzas Among Pines

Pines dressed in white with a wink and a grin,
Whistle a tune, where mischief begins.
Icicles hang like a goofy choir,
Singing off-key, and it's quite the attire.

Snowflakes giggle as they tumble on down,
Creating a quilt that's the talk of the town.
But step too quick, and you'll know it's true,
Snowballs have aims, and they'll target you!

A snowman in shades, looking quite cool,
Is plotting my doom—oh, he's such a fool!
With a top hat askew, he waves with delight,
In this frozen charade, it's a ridiculous sight.

I sipped on my cocoa with marshmallows bright,
As frosty companions joined in the fight.
In this sweet chaos, I won't shed a tear,
For winter's cadenza is all filled with cheer!

Aria of Ice and Silence

Silence hangs thick like a woolly old coat,
But then there's a noise—a snowman's to gloat!
He croaks out an aria, not half-bad at best,
As I join in chorus, my voice in unrest.

With a belly of giggles, I slide on the ice,
Hoping that gravity thinks this is nice.
The pines shake their needles, they're laughing so hard,
As I create music, like a bumbling bard.

Frosted serenades in the hush of the night,
All critters join in, what a curious sight!
The squirrels grab their nuts, tuning up with flair,
Join in the hilarity, if you dare.

So sing with delight, let your voice rise and swell,
In this aria of winter, all's laughter and gel.
For in every freeze, there's a funny twist,
When ice meets the joy, you simply can't resist!

Lament of Winter's Breath

Winter breathes deeply, a frosty old sage,
With a crack and a pop, it releases its rage.
Snowflakes tumble, like clowns in a show,
While I run for cover from their icy throw.

Chattering teeth, they join in the song,
As I hop in the snow, feeling utterly wrong.
Where's my warm cocoa? Where's my fine hat?
Trade 'em for this? Oh, where's my pet cat?

The trees chuckle loudly, their branches all sway,
As I try to dance, but I slip on the way.
Why does winter mock? This season is bold,
Yet every cold moment turns laughter to gold.

So here's to the chill, the snowflakes, the fun,
For winter's lament has only begun.
We'll clap and we'll cheer, despite frozen skin,
For joy hides in laughter, let the chaos begin!

Melody of the Snowbound Silence

Flakes tumble down with a comic twist,
They dance on roofs, they can't resist.
A snowman's nose is a carrot so bright,
He winks at the kids, what a silly sight!

Chasing to catch a dusting of white,
Land face-first, oh, what a delight!
Snowballs are flying, but why's he so slow?
He slips on the ground, what a frosty show!

Mittens so big, they hardly fit,
He's making snow angels—what a perfect hit!
Laughter erupts from the hilltop's embrace,
As snowflakes spin down, they join the race!

A sleigh ride follows, what a robust thrill,
Hooves stomp the ground, a cozy chill.
Hot cocoa steams, a marshmallow crown,
Cheers echo through this frosty town!

Sighs of the Biting Air

Nature's joke as the chill takes hold,
Even the sun seems a bit too bold.
Socks mismatched, a fashion faux pas,
Puffing out cheeks, look at the bizarre!

Huddled together, a bundle of fluff,
Critters in hats, aren't they tough?
Chattering teeth in a comical lull,
Who knew the cold could be so dull?

Ice on the window, a jasper art,
Oh! A squirrel slips, that's just the start.
It's a circus out here, what a funny scene,
As penguins on ice look vaguely obscene.

Breath visible, puffs like a train's,
Races ensue, and there's no one to reign.
Rolling down hills with a giggle and cheer,
Winter's embrace is the best time of year!

Crooning of the Crystal Lattice

Frosty patterns twirl on glass,
Tickling noses as they pass.
Gloves upside down, can you believe?
What an outfit! He's hard to perceive.

Icicles hanging like chandelier lights,
Gleaming in sun, such spectacular sights.
But one falls down, "Oops! Sorry, folks!"
It's just a prank from the snowy blokes!

Laughter erupts as patches of ice,
Send everyone sliding, oh, isn't it nice?
A twirl and a spin, arms flailing wide,
The ground becomes a frosty slide!

Snowflakes giggle like they're on a spree,
Dancing and swirling—pure jubilee.
With every tumble, a chuckle rings clear,
It's wintertime mischief—let's bring on the cheer!

Breath of the Snow-laden Night

Stars twinkle above in a snowy embrace,
Wandering gnomes with a curious pace.
Chill in the air, but spirits are bright,
Decked out in laughter, all through the night.

Snowmen gossip as shadows unfold,
With laughter so boisterous and stories so bold.
They compete in a dance—who can move best?
A jig in the moonlight, forget all the rest!

Noses so rosy, cheeks round and ripe,
Twirls in the snowfall, oh, what a hype!
With cocoa in hand, they take to the street,
Sledding shenanigans, they can't be beat!

As night quietly whispers, stars blink with glee,
It's a magical evening, and all are carefree.
The crackle of laughter, the joy in a sigh,
In this snowy wonderland, spirits fly high!

Dissonance in the Frozen Realm

Snowflakes dance, with socks mismatched,
A penguin slips, oh, what a catch!
The trees wear coats, but not quite right,
They shiver, oh so cold tonight.

The rabbits hop, in boots too tight,
They look like clowns, a funny sight!
The chilly air brings giggles loud,
As everyone falls, it's quite the crowd.

Frosty winks at the sun's sly grin,
While ice cubes race, who'll win, who'll win?
The snowman sneezes, brave and bold,
His carrot nose turns bright and cold.

In this frozen land of frosty joy,
Each slip and trip adds to the ploy;
So grab your hats and join the fun,
In the frosty realm, we've just begun!

The Frost's Embrace

Chilly breezes tickle the toes,
While icicles dangle, watch out, they pose!
Hot cocoa spills as laughter erupts,
In this frosty realm, mischief interrupts.

Snowflakes pile on noses and cheeks,
The ice rink's filled with wobbly freaks.
A cat in boots skids on by,
With a wink and a flip, oh my, oh my!

Gloves are missing, scarves gone astray,
Who wore the last drip from the bay?
In winter's clutch, the goofballs reign,
While snowmen giggle, round the terrain.

With tumbling friends and rosy noses,
The chilly air brings jokes and poses.
So let's embrace this frosty race,
And laugh together in this crazy place!

Shimmering Silence of the Icebound

Silence sparkles, a disco ball,
While polar bears host a snowy brawl.
Penguins juggle with fish on ice,
Their flippers clapping, oh, so nice!

A seal pops up, with a big old grin,
Yells, "Let's slide! Let the chaos begin!"
While snowflakes fall and catch my nose,
I try to catch one, it giggles and goes.

Jack Frost chuckles from his tree,
As skiers tumble, just wait and see.
With boots too big and laughter loud,
We make our way through frosty shroud.

In this glistening land of fun and cheer,
We dance with the snowflakes, never fear!
So grab your friends and join the dance,
In this icy world, give fun a chance!

Serenade of the Chilly Night

Stars twinkle brightly, what a sight,
As squirrels nap, all snug and tight.
The moon plays tunes, soft and sweet,
While happy squirrels tap their feet.

A snowball fight turns into a show,
With mighty laughs and slips in tow.
Snowmen debate, who wears it best,
They take a poll, in their frosty jest.

Frosted cakes, with snow on top,
But wait, who's eating? It's a hop!
A penguin sneaks, ever so sly,
And steals a bite with a cheeky cry.

So let us revel in these frosty days,
With laughter echoing in silly ways.
When cold winds blow and we all sing,
The chilly night is a funny thing!

Eulogy for the Autumn Leaves

Oh, leaves that danced with joy in the breeze,
You thought you'd linger, but with such ease.
Whirling in circles, you fell with a thud,
Leaving folks wondering, 'Was that just a dud?'

Your brilliant colors, a fiery display,
Now crumpled and brown, you've gone quite astray.
With every gust, you flutter and spin,
But we know, dear leaves, this isn't your win!

We salute your departure, so bold and bright,
Though gathered in piles, you put up a fight.
Squirrels conspire, to jump and to play,
As we mourn the leaves that just drifted away.

So let us all chuckle, and raise up a toast,
To leaves that once dazzled, we'll laugh and we'll boast.
For every goodbye is a reason to cheer,
As winter arrives, the snowflakes appear!

Notes of the Crystal Cold

The air is crisp, like a frosty embrace,
With noses all red, and smiles on each face.
Snowflakes descend like confetti from high,
Making us giggle as they float from the sky.

Children are bundled, like sausages round,
Tumbling and rolling, delightfully bound.
They build up the snowmen, quite funny in shape,
With buttons and carrots, a whimsical tape.

The chill in the air sends our breath in a dance,
Chattering teeth as we slip and we prance.
Hot cocoa awaits in our warming abode,
A sweet little potion for frostbitten code.

So sing out your laughter, let joy take the lead,
As winter provides silly moments indeed.
In puddles of snow, we eternally play,
Embracing the cold in the most cheerful way!

Accompaniment of the Frosty Air

Here comes the chill, with a tickle and tease,
It wraps around us like a cold, furry sneeze.
Our hats fly away like unpredictable jokers,
As the frostbitten breeze plays tricks on the folks.

Puffs of white clouds escape from our lips,
Turning into laughter, as we dance and do flips.
We bundle up tight in our layers oh-so-fine,
While looking like marshmallows, we'll sparkle and shine.

Brrr… is the sound that echoes with glee,
As fingers turn numb, but we're as happy as can be.
Snowball fights break out with giggles and yelps,
Who knew that winter would bring out such kelps?

So huddle together, and don't forget your cheer,
For frosty companions bring warmth, never fear.
As we swirl and we twirl, on this ice-laden stage,
Let the music of winter be the best kind of age!

Grail of the Northern Whispers

Listen closely, for whispers arise,
From the chilly north, under overcast skies.
They tickle your ears with a blend of delight,
Bringing shivers and giggles, a marvelous sight.

In quietest corners, they rustle and play,
Like tiny elves scheming to run off and sway.
With branches that creak, and snow softly crunch,
The secrets of winter beg us to munch.

Mittens and scarves dance in treacherous winds,
While everyone's trying to outmaneuver sins.
The ice on the pond tells tales of faux skates,
As we tumble and giggle, at our own silly fates.

So grab on to joy, let it sparkle and sing,
For winter's whispers can bring such a fling.
A grail overflowing with laughter and mirth,
In the heart of the cold, lies the warmth of our worth!

Whispers of the Frosty Breeze

The frosty breeze has quite a laugh,
It tickles trees and steals your scarf.
A sneeze that echoes through the air,
And yet, it dances without a care.

It spins the flakes in joyful jest,
Like little sprites, they twirl and rest.
The chill will make you stomp and shout,
But watch your step, or you might pout.

Old man Winter tells a pun,
As all the animals start to run.
He's got a joke for every season,
That leaves us all without a reason.

With snowflakes glimmering like a show,
The breeze just chuckles, don't you know?
So laugh along with frosty friends,
This chilly fun never really ends.

Echoes in the Silent Snow

The silent snow is quite a tease,
It whispers jokes with every breeze.
A fluffy laugh, it puffs and plays,
And leaves you grinning for days and days.

In snowmen hats with crooked smiles,
They share their jokes across the miles.
So warm your hearts, take off that frown,
Join in the mirth that's snowing down.

Each flake that falls is like a rhyme,
It spins around, it takes its time.
In icy theater, shivers cheer,
As laughter dances, crystal clear.

Just watch your step, be not a fool,
Or end up slipping, oh, what a tool!
With echoes ringing through the night,
Let's revel in this snowy light.

Chilling Melodies of the Night

The night sings loud with icy tones,
A chorus made of chilly groans.
You might just freeze if you stand still,
While caroling trees shout, 'What a thrill!'

With every gust comes laughter wild,
The stars are giggling, oh, how they smiled!
As winter critters join the fun,
A raccoon winks, 'I'm not the one!'

The moon shines bright, an audience gleams,
As breezes tickle all our dreams.
Icy notes fly, they dip and sway,
Who knew that frost could dance this way?

So grab your friends, in jackets wrapped,
And sing along, don't get trapped!
In chilling melodies, laughter flows,
As winter's humor gently grows.

Lullabies of the Icy Gale

The icy gale hums soft and low,
Serenading all the world below.
Each whispered tune is wrapped in ice,
Bringing giggles, oh so nice!

With each cool breeze and snowy wink,
The world gets playful, don't you think?
A melody that stirs the trees,
While critters dance with efforts to please.

It breezes by with clever quips,
Tickling noses, teasing lips.
So bundle up to hear the song,
Where laughter lives and all belong.

When shadows stretch and night descends,
The gale just laughs and never ends.
With cuddly air and frosty play,
Lullabies sing the night away.

Secrets in the Snowdrift's Heart

In snowdrifts deep, the secrets lie,
A squirrel in boots, giving a try.
He slides with flair, a comical twist,
Chasing his tail, he can't resist.

A penguin waltz on frostbit toes,
While snowflakes giggle, nobody knows.
They curl and twirl, a dance out there,
As winter whispers without a care.

The sun peeks through with a cheeky grin,
Reflecting off ice; let the games begin!
A snowman's hat flies up in the breeze,
His carrot nose's lost—oh, what a tease!

So gather 'round, let laughter flow,
In winter's grip, the mirth will grow.
For in the chills, a warmth does start,
There's joy hidden in the snowdrift's heart.

Frosty Serenades at Twilight

As twilight falls with a frosty spark,
The critters gather 'round in the park.
A rabbit strums on a snowy flute,
While a badger hums in his cozy suit.

The stars come out in a playful race,
With polar bears dancing in their space.
They trip and tumble on frozen grounds,
While giggles echo all around.

An owl takes charge of the festive tune,
Singing softly at the light of the moon.
The snowflakes fall, like whispers bright,
Creating joy in the chilly night.

With every note, their hearts ignite,
In frosty serenades, pure delight.
Nature joins in, with laughter and cheer,
As winter's chorus sings loud and clear.

Rhythms of the Bitter Cold

The air is crisp, a chilly delight,
Where icicles sport in the morning light.
A dog in boots hops, seeking his ball,
While snowmen giggle, having a ball!

Footprints left in a zigzag spree,
A snowball flurry, just wait and see!
With each toss, a goal in the snowy field,
To the laughter of friends, no secrets concealed.

A polar bear fumbles, slips on a sled,
His fluffy behind, now blue and red.
The frost might nip, but smiles abound,
In the rhythms of cold, joy can be found.

So come join the dance, let the fun unfold,
In the heart of winter, we're young and bold.
Together we sing, with hearts so free,
For the rhythms of cold are the best, agree?

Harmony of Fragments in Ice

In the heart of winter, fragments play,
Icicles dance in a silly ballet.
Snowflakes giggle as they swirl and spin,
Juggling their patterns; oh, let the fun begin!

A snow squirrel dons his fluffy attire,
Building a snow fort; he's ready for fire!
With marshmallow bombs made of sweet fluff,
He lobs them at birds—oh, is that enough?

A moose in a scarf starts a slow jig,
With rhymes and beats, he's not too big.
The snowdrifts warm from all of the fun,
In harmony's grasp, winter's never done.

So gather your friends, let your spirits lift,
In fragments of ice, find the funniest gift.
For in this cold, where laughter is found,
The harmony of winter is always around.

Memory of Frosted Footsteps

Tiny toes on frozen ground,
Little giggles all around.
Snowballs fly without a care,
Laughter echoes through the air.

Sleds are racing down the lane,
Checkered hats in icy rain.
Chasing snowflakes as they spin,
Who knew winter had such a grin?

Whispers of a snowman's fate,
With a carrot nose, it's first-rate!
But when the sun begins to peek,
Our frosty friend begins to leak.

Puddles form where laughter stood,
Sprinkling joy like winter's wood.
In the frost, we find our cheer,
Funny moments, held so dear.

Reverberating Chill of the Night

The moon laughs with a shimmery glare,
As frosty creatures dance with flair.
Snowmen gossip, twist with glee,
While icicles dangle like jewelry.

Hot cocoa warms both heart and hand,
Mischief lurks in every strand.
Sippin' joy with marshmallow cheer,
Hoping winter's antics stay near.

Snowflakes tickle noses bright,
Howling jokes in the chilly night.
Giggles echo, spirits light,
Chillin' out feels just right.

The silence of the night is grand,
Yet laughter bubbles through the land.
With chilly pranks and playful schemes,
Winter's giggles fill our dreams.

Harmonizing Whispers of the Cold

A frosty breeze plays hide and seek,
With silly hats atop each peak.
Winds that whistle, teasing so,
Bringing smiles wherever they blow.

Snowflakes flutter, each a song,
Filling the air, both bright and strong.
The chilly breeze hums a tune,
Inviting all to dance by moon.

Trees wear gowns of fluff and white,
What a sight, oh what a night!
With winter's music in the air,
We twirl and twirl without a care.

Frosted branches sway and bend,
Nature's laughter knows no end.
In the cold, we gather tight,
Creating joy in winter's light.

Dreamers in the Wintry Mist

Fuzzy mittens on our hands,
Building dreams in snowy lands.
Here a snowball, there a fling,
Winter's magic makes us sing.

Fluffy clouds hang low and round,
Whisper secrets without a sound.
Hot cocoa spills in playful zest,
Life's so funny at its best!

For every slip and tumble down,
We laugh aloud, no need to frown.
Frosty footprints in a line,
Making merry, feeling fine.

As the world turns white and bright,
We dream together, pure delight.
In the mist, we find our play,
Winter's joy will always stay.

Rhapsody of the Frostbitten

Oh frostbite's nippy, chilly tease,
A penguin's waddle brings a breeze.
Snowflakes dance like they're in a race,
Slides and slips with a smiling face.

The carrots stick out on snowmen tall,
Their button eyes shine, but they soon fall.
Hot cocoa spills on mittens tight,
Mugs turn to penguins — what a sight!

Sleds zoom down with laughter galore,
A face-first landing? You'll beg for more!
Snowball fights ignite the frozen field,
From frostbitten foes, we shall not yield!

As the sun sets on this snowy show,
The chilly chaos puts on a glow.
So bundle up, embrace the fun,
For winter plays till the day is done.

Chilling Echoes of Dusk

A frosty whisper flies with flair,
As mittens vanish in frosty air.
Snowflakes tumble with giggles bright,
Frosty breath forms a ghostly light.

Hot dogs wrapped in blankets snug,
While icy toes play tag with a bug.
Chill out, they say, but it's quite fun,
We'll run and skit 'til the day is done.

Candles flicker in the brisk night chill,
When icicles dangle, you know the drill.
With each crackle, we dance by the fire,
But step too close and you'll meet the choir!

So laugh at frost, let your spirits rise,
For winter's pranks are a wild surprise.
Echoing through, the chuckles float,
In twilight's grip, we'll find our note.

Harmony of the Arctic Shadows

In the shadows where snowflakes play,
The arctic critters keep boredom at bay.
A moose with shades struts proud and slow,
While rabbits make snow angels in a row.

Snowball dodging from a dainty hare,
Who steals a carrot without a care.
An owl swings by with a hoot and a wink,
As winter's got all the creatures in sync.

With frosty whiskers and laughs that freeze,
The orchestra plays with a chilly breeze.
Frosty fingers tap a little tune,
Under the stars and a frosted moon.

So gather 'round as shadows look on,
The harmony of winter feels like a song.
Let's twirl and leap in this frosty delight,
For we're the stars in the snowy night.

Whispering Pines in the Cold

Whispers through pine trees, oh what a sight!
A squirrel in boots dancing left and right.
With acorns that scatter like tossed confetti,
He's ready for fun — oh, aren't we all ready?

A snowman's hat blows away with a laugh,
While kids make a pact for the sledding path.
With cheeks rosy red, they yell, "All aboard!"
And off they go, laughing without a cord.

As snowflakes whisper secrets to all,
The trees start to chuckle, they're having a ball.
On frozen ponds, ice skaters flaunt,
With twirls and slips like a festive jaunt.

So let's toast marshmallows by campfire glow,
While the pines sway gently, secrets they know.
Embrace the chill and the giggles it brings,
For winter's a canvas where laughter sings.

Harmony in the Chill of Evening

In the frosty air, a squirrel did prance,
Wearing tiny boots, he took a chance.
Sliding on ice, he fell with a thud,
Then shook off his coat, covered in mud.

Snowflakes danced like a playful jest,
Tickling noses, they do their best.
Children laughing, their cheeks all aglow,
Chasing each other through fields of snow.

A snowman wobbles, a carrot for a nose,
He sneezes loudly, and off his hat goes!
The dogs all bark; they're ready to pounce,
At a gang of snowballs they hope to flounce.

As the evening comes, with stars all agleam,
Hot cocoa waiting, a fluffy whipped cream.
Let's gather round for a warm, silly chat,
Telling tales of the time our snowman fell flat.

Beneath a Shroud of Frost

Underneath the frost, the rabbits are spry,
With scarves and mittens, they hop and fly.
Mischief abounds in the snowy white haze,
Snatching lost hats in a playful craze.

A penguin slips on the icy slick ground,
Doing a dance, makes everyone sound.
Laughter erupts as he tumbles away,
Poor little fella, what a clumsy display!

Icicles hang like the world's sharpest tooth,
A snowball fight breaks out, oh what a sleuth!
Dodging and weaving, they laugh in delight,
Making snow angels until it's goodnight.

As stars start to twinkle, and shadows grow long,
We gather close, singing our favorite song.
In this frosty land, with joy and with cheer,
We cherish the moments, as winter draws near.

Songs of the Glistening Twilight

Twilight glistens with a shine so bright,
While owls plan a party, oh what a sight!
They're hooting and tooting, they're waiting for fun,
Inviting the critters, as day's nearly done.

Beneath the moon glow, the snowflakes twirl,
A flurry of giggles in a frosty whirl.
A fox in a bowtie, quite dapper and neat,
Tripped over his tail and fell at the feet!

Snowmen and snow-women warm up for a ball,
With buttons and smiles, they stand proud and tall.
Yet one did a jig, then collapsed with a groan,
Dreaming of summers, their melting time shown.

As laughter erupts through the chilly air,
Our hearts feel the warmth of this glistening fair.
With joy in the twilight, let's sing through the night,
For winter's a wonder, and this feels just right!

The Lament of the Evergreen

A lonely pine tree in a field so wide,
Misses its needles, they've lost their pride.
A family of rabbits has claimed the best spots,
Sipping on sap from his slushy green knots.

The breeze plays a tune through branches so bare,
Whispering secrets of winter's cold stare.
"Oh where are my friends?" the evergreen sighs,
"Maybe they're frozen or lost in the skies!"

A squirrel named Benny bursts through the fluff,
"I've no time to chat, I'm far too tough!"
He races on by with a nut in his mouth,
While the tree just chuckles, "Ah, winter's cold South."

As night falls around in a blanket of white,
The evergreen chuckles, "What a silly sight!
Though needles may fade, and the branches may groan,
In this winter tale, I'll never be alone!"

Murmurs Beneath the Snowy Veil

Snowflakes whisper secrets, oh so light,
They tickle our noses, what a silly sight.
With mittens and boots, we stomp and we play,
While the snowmen chuckle, they brightened our day.

Hot cocoa in hand, we sip and we grin,
The marshmallows float, like a fluffy win.
With a flick of the wrist, a snowball takes flight,
But the dog catches it, what a comical plight!

The Dance of Arctic Shadows

Shadows prance to the tune of the snow,
Where penguins in bow ties put on quite a show.
Icicles shimmer like disco balls bright,
As snowflakes do waltz in the pale moonlight.

Frosty the snowman, a danseur supreme,
In a flurry of giggles, he twirls in a dream.
While the cat in the window, bemused by it all,
Sips on hot chocolate, just waiting to sprawl.

Notes Carried by the Frigid Air

The chilly breeze hums a merry old tune,
Chasing off squirrels who scatter too soon.
As coffee mugs clatter, we giggle and cheer,
At the sight of a snowman with no nose in fear.

A gust plays a trick, the hats fly like planes,
In the snowy white chaos, laughter remains.
With sleds made of laughter, we glide down so fast,
While the snow piles high, making memories last.

Ballad of the Silent Pines

Silent pines sway gently, in a frozen sway,
While squirrels in sweaters make mischief, hooray!
The branches all giggle, they shake with surprise,
As snowflakes tickle them, right in their eyes.

A raccoon with a scarf plays peek-a-boo bliss,
While critters in snowmen share their holiday wish.
In the hush of the woods, a chorus takes flight,
As nature joins in for this frosty delight!

Serenade in the Frozen Air

A snowflake sneezed, oh what a sight,
It tumbled down in pure delight.
The trees all giggled, branches swayed,
As socks on cats in winter played.

The ice was slippery, me with flair,
I skated past a dancing bear.
He twirled and slipped with all his might,
And gave a sigh, what a frozen night!

The chill in the air, not so serious,
The rabbits hopped, all so curious.
They wore little hats, oh such a joke,
As winter's laughter began to poke.

Now snowmen grinned with carrot noses,
While penguins strutted in fancy poses.
In this frosty world, we sing and play,
Making merry in our own silly way.

Breath of the Crystal Whirl

A chilly puff, like a breath of frost,
Whisked by a squirrel, who felt quite lost.
It tickled his tail, made him spin,
He danced on the ice with a cheeky grin.

The snowflakes fell, their dance a tease,
Whirling 'round trees, like buzzing bees.
A snowman sneezed, and then he swayed,
As winter's goofiness was displayed.

See the deer wearing funny vests,
Trying to jump in uncoordinated quests.
They laugh as they trip, in league with the breeze,
In this frosty world, they do as they please.

With each chilly gust, there's laughter and cheer,
As snowball fights start to draw near.
We spin and we twirl, in this frosty fun,
In winter's wild state, we're never outdone.

Haunting Harmonies of December

In December's chill, a howling tune,
Brought joy to the light of a silvery moon.
The owls hooted loud, the rabbits danced,
In this winter wonder, all creatures pranced.

Icicles hung like teeth of a grin,
As birds chirped songs under snow's soft skin.
A raccoon played drums on trash can tops,
Creating a beat that just never stops.

The breezes joked with each fluffy flake,
While you could hear the snowmen quake.
With noses so bright and smiles so wide,
They'd share the fun, come join the ride!

Each gust of air brings chuckles loud,
As winter wraps all in a giggling shroud.
Let's raise a glass to frosty foes,
In this playful frost, we know how it goes.

Frosted Tunes of Nature's Breath

The air sings soft, like sweet cotton candy,
And snowflakes swirl, a dance quite dandy.
The rabbits race with squirrels so spry,
While snowmen wave, oh my, oh my!

A puff of wind sends hats a-flying,
While everyone else is just trying!
To catch their mittens in the cold blue,
Oh, let's not forget the tasty stew!

Frosted trees wear sparkly whites,
While birds on branches have funny fights.
They chirp and twirl in merry glee,
As winter sings its song, oh whee!

So here's to the fun within the freeze,
To bonfires, marshmallows, and snowy trees.
In each flurry and flake, we find our joy,
A dance in the cold for every girl and boy.

Milton Keynes UK
Ingram Content Group UK Ltd.
UKHW022342171124
451242UK00007B/102

9 789916 946008